THIS JOURNAL BELONGS TO:

....

- 👤
- 📞
- @
- 📍

DATE: ....

LOCATION: ....
WEATHER: ....
GEAR USED: ....
SETTINGS: ....

 **TREASURES FOUND THIS DAY**

ITEMS FOUND	GPS/LOCATION	TIME	ESTIMATED VALUE

NOTES

SKETCH

DATE: ....

LOCATION: ....

WEATHER: ....

GEAR USED: ....

SETTINGS: ....

 **TREASURES FOUND THIS DAY**

ITEMS FOUND	GPS/LOCATION	TIME	ESTIMATED VALUE

NOTES

SKETCH

DATE: ....

LOCATION: ....
WEATHER: ....
GEAR USED: ....
SETTINGS: ....

 **TREASURES FOUND THIS DAY**

ITEMS FOUND	GPS/LOCATION	TIME	ESTIMATED VALUE

NOTES

SKETCH

DATE: ....

LOCATION: ....
WEATHER: ....
GEAR USED: ....
SETTINGS: ....

 TREASURES FOUND THIS DAY

ITEMS FOUND	GPS/LOCATION	TIME	ESTIMATED VALUE

NOTES

SKETCH

DATE: ....

LOCATION: ....
WEATHER: ....
GEAR USED: ....
SETTINGS: ....

TREASURES FOUND THIS DAY

ITEMS FOUND	GPS/LOCATION	TIME	ESTIMATED VALUE

NOTES

SKETCH

DATE: ....

LOCATION: ....
WEATHER: ....
GEAR USED: ....
SETTINGS: ....

 TREASURES FOUND THIS DAY

ITEMS FOUND	GPS/LOCATION	TIME	ESTIMATED VALUE

NOTES

SKETCH

DATE: ....

LOCATION: ....

WEATHER: ....

GEAR USED: ....

SETTINGS: ....

 **TREASURES FOUND THIS DAY**

ITEMS FOUND	GPS/LOCATION	TIME	ESTIMATED VALUE

NOTES

SKETCH

DATE: ....

LOCATION: ....
WEATHER: ....
GEAR USED: ....
SETTINGS: ....

TREASURES FOUND THIS DAY

ITEMS FOUND	GPS/LOCATION	TIME	ESTIMATED VALUE

NOTES

SKETCH

DATE: ....

LOCATION: ....

WEATHER: ....

GEAR USED: ....

SETTINGS: ....

 **TREASURES FOUND THIS DAY**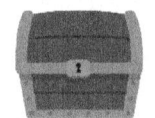

ITEMS FOUND	GPS/LOCATION	TIME	ESTIMATED VALUE

NOTES

SKETCH

DATE: ....

LOCATION: ....

WEATHER: ....

GEAR USED: ....

SETTINGS: ....

 **TREASURES FOUND THIS DAY**

ITEMS FOUND	GPS/LOCATION	TIME	ESTIMATED VALUE

NOTES

SKETCH

DATE: ....

LOCATION: ....
WEATHER: ....
GEAR USED: ....
SETTINGS: ....

TREASURES FOUND THIS DAY

ITEMS FOUND	GPS/LOCATION	TIME	ESTIMATED VALUE

NOTES

SKETCH

DATE: ....

LOCATION: ....
WEATHER: ....
GEAR USED: ....
SETTINGS: ....

 **TREASURES FOUND THIS DAY**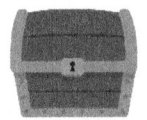

ITEMS FOUND	GPS/LOCATION	TIME	ESTIMATED VALUE

NOTES

SKETCH

DATE: ....

LOCATION: ....
WEATHER: ....
GEAR USED: ....
SETTINGS: ....

 **TREASURES FOUND THIS DAY**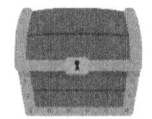

ITEMS FOUND	GPS/LOCATION	TIME	ESTIMATED VALUE

NOTES

SKETCH

DATE: ....

LOCATION: ....
WEATHER: ....
GEAR USED: ....
SETTINGS: ....

TREASURES FOUND THIS DAY

ITEMS FOUND	GPS/LOCATION	TIME	ESTIMATED VALUE

NOTES

SKETCH

DATE: ....

LOCATION: ....
WEATHER: ....
GEAR USED: ....
SETTINGS: ....

 **TREASURES FOUND THIS DAY**

ITEMS FOUND	GPS/LOCATION	TIME	ESTIMATED VALUE

NOTES

SKETCH

DATE: ....

LOCATION: ....

WEATHER: ....

GEAR USED: ....

SETTINGS: ....

 **TREASURES FOUND THIS DAY**

ITEMS FOUND	GPS/LOCATION	TIME	ESTIMATED VALUE

NOTES

SKETCH

DATE: ....

LOCATION: ....
WEATHER: ....
GEAR USED: ....
SETTINGS: ....

TREASURES FOUND THIS DAY

ITEMS FOUND	GPS/LOCATION	TIME	ESTIMATED VALUE

NOTES

SKETCH

DATE: ....

LOCATION: ....
WEATHER: ....
GEAR USED: ....
SETTINGS: ....

 **TREASURES FOUND THIS DAY**

ITEMS FOUND	GPS/LOCATION	TIME	ESTIMATED VALUE

NOTES

SKETCH

DATE: ....

LOCATION: ....

WEATHER: ....

GEAR USED: ....

SETTINGS: ....

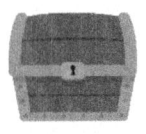 TREASURES FOUND THIS DAY

ITEMS FOUND	GPS/LOCATION	TIME	ESTIMATED VALUE

NOTES

SKETCH

DATE: ....

LOCATION: ....
WEATHER: ....
GEAR USED: ....
SETTINGS: ....

TREASURES FOUND THIS DAY

ITEMS FOUND	GPS/LOCATION	TIME	ESTIMATED VALUE

NOTES

SKETCH

DATE: ....

LOCATION: ....
WEATHER: ....
GEAR USED: ....
SETTINGS: ....

 **TREASURES FOUND THIS DAY**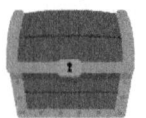

ITEMS FOUND	GPS/LOCATION	TIME	ESTIMATED VALUE

NOTES

SKETCH

DATE: ......

LOCATION: ......
WEATHER: ......
GEAR USED: ......
SETTINGS: ......

 **TREASURES FOUND THIS DAY**

ITEMS FOUND	GPS/LOCATION	TIME	ESTIMATED VALUE

NOTES

SKETCH

DATE: ....

LOCATION: ....
WEATHER: ....
GEAR USED: ....
SETTINGS: ....

TREASURES FOUND THIS DAY

ITEMS FOUND	GPS/LOCATION	TIME	ESTIMATED VALUE

NOTES

SKETCH

DATE: ....

LOCATION: ....
WEATHER: ....
GEAR USED: ....
SETTINGS: ....

 **TREASURES FOUND THIS DAY**

ITEMS FOUND	GPS/LOCATION	TIME	ESTIMATED VALUE

NOTES

SKETCH

DATE: ....

LOCATION: ....
WEATHER: ....
GEAR USED: ....
SETTINGS: ....

 **TREASURES FOUND THIS DAY**

ITEMS FOUND	GPS/LOCATION	TIME	ESTIMATED VALUE

NOTES

SKETCH

DATE: ....

LOCATION: ....
WEATHER: ....
GEAR USED: ....
SETTINGS: ....

TREASURES FOUND THIS DAY

ITEMS FOUND	GPS/LOCATION	TIME	ESTIMATED VALUE

NOTES

SKETCH

DATE: ....

LOCATION: ....
WEATHER: ....
GEAR USED: ....
SETTINGS: ....

 **TREASURES FOUND THIS DAY**

ITEMS FOUND	GPS/LOCATION	TIME	ESTIMATED VALUE

NOTES

SKETCH

DATE: ....

LOCATION: ....

WEATHER: ....

GEAR USED: ....

SETTINGS: ....

 **TREASURES FOUND THIS DAY**

ITEMS FOUND	GPS/LOCATION	TIME	ESTIMATED VALUE

NOTES

SKETCH

DATE: ....

LOCATION: ....
WEATHER: ....
GEAR USED: ....
SETTINGS: ....

TREASURES FOUND THIS DAY

ITEMS FOUND	GPS/LOCATION	TIME	ESTIMATED VALUE

NOTES

SKETCH

DATE: ....

LOCATION: ....
WEATHER: ....
GEAR USED: ....
SETTINGS: ....

 **TREASURES FOUND THIS DAY**

ITEMS FOUND	GPS/LOCATION	TIME	ESTIMATED VALUE

NOTES

SKETCH

DATE: ....

LOCATION: ....
WEATHER: ....
GEAR USED: ....
SETTINGS: ....

 **TREASURES FOUND THIS DAY**

ITEMS FOUND	GPS/LOCATION	TIME	ESTIMATED VALUE

NOTES

SKETCH

DATE: ....

LOCATION: ....

WEATHER: ....

GEAR USED: ....

SETTINGS: ....

TREASURES FOUND THIS DAY

ITEMS FOUND	GPS/LOCATION	TIME	ESTIMATED VALUE

NOTES

SKETCH

DATE: ....

LOCATION: ....
WEATHER: ....
GEAR USED: ....
SETTINGS: ....

 TREASURES FOUND THIS DAY

ITEMS FOUND	GPS/LOCATION	TIME	ESTIMATED VALUE

NOTES

SKETCH

DATE: ....

LOCATION: ....

WEATHER: ....

GEAR USED: ....

SETTINGS: ....

 **TREASURES FOUND THIS DAY**

ITEMS FOUND	GPS/LOCATION	TIME	ESTIMATED VALUE

NOTES

SKETCH

DATE: ....

LOCATION: ....

WEATHER: ....

GEAR USED: ....

SETTINGS: ....

TREASURES FOUND THIS DAY

ITEMS FOUND	GPS/LOCATION	TIME	ESTIMATED VALUE

NOTES

SKETCH

DATE: ....

LOCATION: ....

WEATHER: ....

GEAR USED: ....

SETTINGS: ....

 TREASURES FOUND THIS DAY

ITEMS FOUND	GPS/LOCATION	TIME	ESTIMATED VALUE

NOTES

SKETCH

DATE: ....

LOCATION: ....

WEATHER: ....

GEAR USED: ....

SETTINGS: ....

 **TREASURES FOUND THIS DAY**

ITEMS FOUND	GPS/LOCATION	TIME	ESTIMATED VALUE

NOTES

SKETCH

DATE: ....

LOCATION: ....

WEATHER: ....

GEAR USED: ....

SETTINGS: ....

TREASURES FOUND THIS DAY

ITEMS FOUND	GPS/LOCATION	TIME	ESTIMATED VALUE

NOTES

SKETCH

DATE: ....

LOCATION: ....
WEATHER: ....
GEAR USED: ....
SETTINGS: ....

 **TREASURES FOUND THIS DAY**

ITEMS FOUND	GPS/LOCATION	TIME	ESTIMATED VALUE

NOTES

SKETCH

DATE: ....

LOCATION: ....
WEATHER: ....
GEAR USED: ....
SETTINGS: ....

 TREASURES FOUND THIS DAY

ITEMS FOUND	GPS/LOCATION	TIME	ESTIMATED VALUE

NOTES

SKETCH

DATE: ....

LOCATION: ....
WEATHER: ....
GEAR USED: ....
SETTINGS: ....

TREASURES FOUND THIS DAY

ITEMS FOUND	GPS/LOCATION	TIME	ESTIMATED VALUE

NOTES

SKETCH

DATE: ....

LOCATION: ....
WEATHER: ....
GEAR USED: ....
SETTINGS: ....

 **TREASURES FOUND THIS DAY**

ITEMS FOUND	GPS/LOCATION	TIME	ESTIMATED VALUE

NOTES

SKETCH

DATE: ....

LOCATION: ....
WEATHER: ....
GEAR USED: ....
SETTINGS: ....

 TREASURES FOUND THIS DAY

ITEMS FOUND	GPS/LOCATION	TIME	ESTIMATED VALUE

NOTES

SKETCH

DATE: ....

LOCATION: ....

WEATHER: ....

GEAR USED: ....

SETTINGS: ....

TREASURES FOUND THIS DAY

ITEMS FOUND	GPS/LOCATION	TIME	ESTIMATED VALUE

NOTES

SKETCH

DATE: ....

LOCATION: ....
WEATHER: ....
GEAR USED: ....
SETTINGS: ....

 **TREASURES FOUND THIS DAY**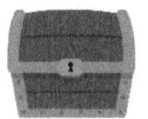

ITEMS FOUND	GPS/LOCATION	TIME	ESTIMATED VALUE

NOTES

SKETCH

DATE: ....

LOCATION: ....
WEATHER: ....
GEAR USED: ....
SETTINGS: ....

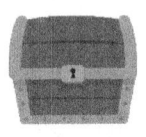 **TREASURES FOUND THIS DAY**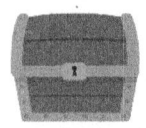

ITEMS FOUND	GPS/LOCATION	TIME	ESTIMATED VALUE

NOTES

....

....

....

....

....

....

....

....

SKETCH

DATE: ....

LOCATION: ....
WEATHER: ....
GEAR USED: ....
SETTINGS: ....

TREASURES FOUND THIS DAY

ITEMS FOUND	GPS/LOCATION	TIME	ESTIMATED VALUE

NOTES

SKETCH

DATE: ....

LOCATION: ....
WEATHER: ....
GEAR USED: ....
SETTINGS: ....

 **TREASURES FOUND THIS DAY**

ITEMS FOUND	GPS/LOCATION	TIME	ESTIMATED VALUE

NOTES

SKETCH

DATE: ....

LOCATION: ....
WEATHER: ....
GEAR USED: ....
SETTINGS: ....

 TREASURES FOUND THIS DAY

ITEMS FOUND	GPS/LOCATION	TIME	ESTIMATED VALUE

NOTES

SKETCH

DATE: ....

LOCATION: ....
WEATHER: ....
GEAR USED: ....
SETTINGS: ....

TREASURES FOUND THIS DAY

ITEMS FOUND	GPS/LOCATION	TIME	ESTIMATED VALUE

NOTES

SKETCH

Printed in Great Britain
by Amazon